ATLANTA

ATLANTA

Introduction by
Maynard Holbrook Jackson
Mayor of Atlanta, 1974–82
Partner, Chapman and Cutler

Photography by
Jane Sobel and Arthur J. Klonsky

SKYLINE PRESS

To Our Friend and Companion
Beauregard

Our special thanks are due to the Omni International Hotel,
Louise Dillard, The Dillard House Inn, David Scott,
Jerry Rainwater, Kip Weathers, Dr Philip Schley, Rod Ratcliffe,
Bob Brennan Senior, The Hartsfield International Airport,
the Coca-Cola Company and Ramada Inns.

Produced by Boulton Publishing Services, Inc., Toronto
Designed by Fortunato Aglialoro

©1985 Oxford University Press (Canadian Branch)
SKYLINE PRESS is a registered imprint of the Oxford University Press

ISBN 0-19-540625-7
1 2 3 4 – 8 7 6 5
Printed in Hong Kong by Scanner Art Services, Inc., Toronto

Also photographed for this series by Jane Sobel and Arthur J. Klonsky
are *New Orleans*, with an introduction by Pete Fountain,
and *A Southern Celebration*, with an introduction by
Christian Gehman.

Introduction

A friend of mine asked me recently what word I thought would best describe Atlanta. I was as surprised as she was when the first word that popped out of my mouth was 'trees.' That's right. *Trees*.

I know it is fashionable these days to talk of streamlined transportation systems and high-tech industries, when describing a city's fine points, and Atlanta has a most impressive list of statistics in these and other critical categories. I know one is expected to speak of economic development and an efficient work force, while quoting from favorable press clippings and enthusiastic travel editors, and our great city qualifies. I know all of that but I still say 'trees.'

There was a time, I will admit, when trees would probably never have crossed my mind. When I was first elected Mayor of Atlanta I was surprised, and just a little bit amused, to find an 'arborist' on my payroll. It was not a job the intense young man who held the position took lightly. Developers with multi-million dollar projects, as well as homeowners with blue-prints for adding a deck out back, learned that part of their planning had to include an acceptable response to the question of what was going to happen to the *trees*.

During the first few months of my administration, the care of our city's trees was taken for granted, like the warmth of our people, or our unshakable pride in 'the Gate City'. Trees were everywhere, like the smiles and good wishes one meets on the streets in the morning, and I rarely gave them an anxious thought.

However, I began to remember my late father's passion for trees, and our shared determination that Atlanta look a little closer *at* the trees and *through* them into the forest.

Atlanta, the capital of the State of Georgia, is a city of contradictions in many ways. Once the hub of The Confederacy, Atlanta in 1974 became the first major Southern city to elect an Afro-American mayor. Long known for its genteel hospitality and firm sense of tradition, Atlanta now is also a bustling, dynamic, trend-setting, international center of finance and commerce, where citizens, aware that Metro-Atlanta is among the fastest growing urban centers in America, will joke that if you leave the city for more than a week you'll find a new skyscraper or two when you get back. A popular stop for tourists and conventioneers from around the nation and from all parts of the world, Atlanta plays host to millions of visitors a year and yet the gleaming towers of our world-famous luxury hotels stand within walking distance of the birthplace and tomb of Dr Martin Luther King, Jr, and the reflective calm of The Martin Luther King, Junior, Center for Nonviolent Social Change. Our central business district is surrounded by some of Atlanta's oldest and most graceful residential neighborhoods, often complete with thriving vegetable- and flower-gardens and expressing the peace and neighborliness you might expect to find only in a town one-tenth our size.

At the end of my second consecutive and, as required by law, final term as Mayor of Atlanta, in the midst of a boom in real estate and economic development, at a time of unprecedented growth, Atlanta was selected by Rand McNalley as *number one in 'quality of life'* among more than 250 American metropolitan urban areas. Our arts programs and our newly expanded arts environment (and our *trees*) helped our rating.

In the 'slow-paced South', we built the world's biggest airport terminal, ahead of schedule and within budget. In the 'traditionally agricultural South', Atlanta has 29 degree-granting colleges and universities and is an industrial, distribution and high-tech leader among Southern cities.

The list goes on. Rather than heightening the contradictions between the real and the expected however, these realities seem, at a certain point, to make the old assumptions unimportant. The fact that so many different moods, landscapes and lifestyles are able not merely to co-exist, but to interact and in the process of that interaction become strengthened and enriched may, in fact, be the key to Atlanta's beauty as well as her strength.

I think that Atlanta's greatness has something to do with our city's unique ability not just to adapt to change but to welcome it. Atlantans have not always approached the future with certainty but we have never approached it with less than curiosity, enthusiasm and confidence, convinced that progress does not mean the abandonment of the old, but the transformation of it into something more dynamic, more challenging, and more suited to our needs as a community.

I do not imply that we have sailed smoothly through the years from our city's founding in 1837, as a railroad crossroads with the unlikely name of 'Terminus', until today when Atlantans continue to struggle to find creative and humane solutions to the same problems that face all of America's urban centers. We have had our ups and downs, our good years and our 'tryin' times'. We have seen seventy per cent of our city burnt to the ground by General Sherman's torches, toward the end of the Civil War. We have sent our soldiers to fight in America's wars and we have mourned our losses. We have suffered through the Depression of the 1930's and we have welcomed the WPA-created jobs. In 1954, with a population of little more than 300,000 people, we grappled with the decision of the Supreme Court that outlawed 'separate but equal', searching and peacefully finding new ways to live and work together as brothers and sisters. During the 1960s and 1970s we felt and controlled the tremors of change that shook this country as we grew creatively to a population of almost half a million in a metropole of almost two million people.

The challenges have been real, the defeats have been intense, the victories have been sweet but what, one may ask, does all of this have to do with those trees about which I rhapsodized a few paragraphs ago? *Everything!* Our trees represent more than a lush, green canopy that cools and shades us. Our trees reflect our beauty, our strength, our resilience as a community of people. The green of Atlanta's trees stands for life, renewal, growth, and beauty. Our trees are a majestic reminder of the fact that we share our space on this earth with other living things, not just with monuments of brick and mortar, concrete and asphalt. Our trees, so green, so evident to tens of millions of airline passengers gliding into Atlanta's airport, offer a gentle counterpart to the hectic hustle of modern urban life. They remind us that *quality* is as critical to a full life as *quantity*.

In the final analysis Atlantans and other Americans now understand better that what makes Atlanta unique is the *quality* of life here. I began to appreciate not just our high-grade municipal bond-ratings, that make us so eagerly welcome in the canyons of Wall Street, but the beauty of our Symphony, playing for free on the lawns of Piedmont Park to massive, respectful audiences of young and old, rich and poor, black and white. We learned to listen as carefully to the voices of our poets and playwrights as we did to our pundits and politicians. We opened our eyes to the wonders of our new Museum and our brightly painted urban murals, as well as making mental notes of a street that needed re-paving or a traffic-signal that was out-of-synch. We took the time to appreciate the exceptional artwork that is everywhere in our busy airport, challenging and inspiring us as we hurry on our journeys.

We learned to walk, and to listen to our neighbors' voices floating from their front porches in greeting as we passed. We learned to see our reflections, not only in the shiny windows of the newest office-complex to cut the ribbon and open its doors to our welcome, but in the eyes of our children—hopeful, loving, confident and eager.

Although I am now in the private practice of law, my feelings about Atlanta have not changed. Like Atlantans generally I love my home town but I am now more aware of how difficult it can be to describe adequately those things that are closest to your heart. I had the privilege of serving Atlanta as Vice-Mayor and then as Mayor, and I confess that I paid for that privilege in loss of sleep, with not enough time for reflection, and with constant interruptions of normal family life. Nevertheless, to be candid, to look deeply into the forest, I freely admit that any sacrifices my family and I made were more than outweighed by the excitement and the deep satisfaction of having played more than a passing part in the life of one of the world's great cities. For that I am grateful to the people of Atlanta, the people I am proud to call my friends and my neighbors, the people who rejoice in growth and who celebrate progress, but continue to take the time to protect and enjoy their *trees*.

Atlanta is that kind of place—where the old and the new, the natural and the human-created, can achieve the balance necessary to complete the total urban picture.

I am sure this book will rekindle pleasant memories of past visits to our city and provide an attraction for future visits to come. When you arrive here you will find us waiting to greet you and to bid you welcome.

MAYNARD HOLBROOK JACKSON

1 Atlanta, seen from Stone Mountain.

2 *(left)* Every year on the Fourth of July some 25,000 runners gather to take part in the six-mile Peachtree Road Race.

3 'Six Flags over Georgia', one of the best theme-parks in the country; 331 acres, over 100 rides, shows and attractions, including the two roller-coasters 'The Mind Bender' (world's only triple-loop) and the 'Great American Scream Machine'.

4 'Georgia Tech, Ramblin' Wreck'; Atlanta is exceptionally rich in higher education, with 19 degree-giving institutions including Emory University (1836), Atlanta University (1865), The Georgia Institute of Technology (1885), and Georgia State University, as well as two dozen business schools, ten vocational schools, several junior colleges and equivalents.

5 *(right)* 'Six Flags over Georgia', with its multitude of shows, rail- and river-rides, free-fall parachuting and the like, is designed also to portray Georgia's history, the six sections of the park being given to the six flags that have flown over Georgia—those of France, Spain, England, the United States, the Confederacy and Georgia herself.

6 'Six Flags over Georgia' (see previous page).

7 White-water run at 'Six Flags over Georgia'.

8 *(left)* Atlanta State Farmers' Market, a large and lively center for fresh fruit and vegetables, home-canned relishes, preserves, farm eggs and smoked meats; covering 146 acres, the Market is one of the largest in the world.

9 Springtime along Habersham Drive.

10 *(left)* High Museum of Art (1983)—High is a family name—an architectural masterpiece by Richard Meier, with 135,000 square feet of museum space, a four-storey atrium, an auditorium, workshops and an educational level; adjacent to the Arts Center.

11 Robert W. Woodruff Arts Center, formerly the Atlanta Memorial Arts Center, built in 1968 entirely by private funds. The Center offers something to all art lovers—the High Museum, the Atlanta Symphony, the Alliance Theatre, the Atlanta Children's Theatre, and the Atlanta College of Art.

12 *(left)* Runners in Oakland Cemetery; established in 1850, this beautiful Victorian cemetery shelters impressive memorials and several famous names (see plate 69).

13 Garden of the Governor's Mansion, West Paces Ferry Road; newly built in 1968 but in a Greek Revival style that recalls the antebellum South. Furnishings include a fine collection from the early 19th century Federal period.

14 Trout-fishing near Dillard.

15 *(right)* White-water rafting on the Chat-
tooga River, North Georgia.

16 The Cyclorama, Grant Park, a 360° panoramic painting in the round, 50 feet high and 400 feet in circumference, three-dimensional in its effect with surrounding light and sound, that recreates the Battle of Atlanta, 1864.

17 *(right)* Stone Mountain Park; on the mountain face is the world's largest relief sculpture, portraying three great leaders of the Confederacy—President Jefferson Davies, General Robert E. Lee and General Thomas J. 'Stonewall' Jackson. Three sculptors took nearly 20 years to carve this monument. Some idea of the scale may be suggested by the fact that Lee's likeness (center) is 138 feet tall. His sword alone is four feet wide by 58 feet long.

18 Fernbank Science Center, with one of the largest planetariums in the world, also comprises natural science exhibits, a major observatory and the 65-acre Fernbank Forest.

19 *(right)* The 'Satellite Dish Garden' at Turner Communications.

20 At Stone Mountain Park a full-size replica of the famous Civil War steam-locomotive 'The General' (the original built in 1855 is in the Big Shanty Museum at Kennesaw, Georgia) pulls vintage coaches several miles around the base of the colossal granite mountain.

21 Eagle sculpture by Elber Weinberg; Atlanta has been the headquarters
of the US Sixth District of the Federal Reserve Bank since creation of the
Federal Reserve System in 1914.

22 Mick's Restaurant, Lenox Square.

23 *(right)* View from Central City Park.

24 Peachtree Center, a complex renowned for its architecture, and comprising four office towers, a three-level mall, several major hotels, and the Atlanta Merchandise Mart and Atlanta Apparel Mart.

25 'The 'Georgia Arch' (1856), University of Georgia, Athens campus.

26 Capital of Georgia since 1868, the 'Gate City of the South' has been so much in the forefront of growth and renaissance since the 1960s that Atlantans already set aside the title 'New York of the South' in favor of 'the Next Great International City'.

27 *(right)* Tower Place.

28 & 29 Stone Mountain Railroad (see also plate 20); other attractions of Stone Mountain Park include the sternwheeler *Henry Grady* on the lake and a 19-building complex, Stone Mountain Village, that reconstructs life on an antebellum plantation.

30 *(left)* The Atlanta Symphony Orchestra performs its main winter concerts in the 1,800-seat Symphony Hall and its winter Pops Concerts at the Fox Theatre (see plate 44).

31 Dailey's Restaurant and Bar, International Boulevard.

32 & 33 Callaway Gardens, Pine Mountain, is 2,500 acres of woodlands, gardens, nature trails and wildflowers, all created by Cason Callaway as a non-profit-making foundation for the enjoyment of the people of Georgia. The gardens include a greenhouse complex, a vegetable garden (7¹/₂ acres), a restored pioneer cabin, a memorial chapel, and a mile-long man-made beach. As many as 75,000 specimens may be planted in a single year, azaleas, rhododendrons, camellias, gardenias, magnolias—there are 600 varieties of azaleas alone. Beginning in the 1930s, Cason Callaway realized his dream, 'to hang the picture a little higher on the wall for the people of this region... Every child ought to see something beautiful before he's six years old.'

34 *(left)* The spectacular 23-storey atrium lobby of the Hyatt Regency, Atlanta, first of the new hotels that turned the center of Atlanta into a cluster of superlatives today.

35 Grant Park contains a restored Confederate battery, Fort Walker, with guns and ammunition positioned as for the Battle of Atlanta, and the Cyclorama of the battle (see plate 16), as well as miles of walks, some along the earthworks built to defend the city in 1864.

36 *(left)* Downtown at sunset.

37 Phoenix sculpture, First National Bank Building.

38 *(left)* The Omni International Megastructure, along with the Peachtree Center one of the astonishing complexes that have made central Atlanta a hub of shopping and commerce.

39 Staircase in the historic Candler Building (1920), built as the home of Charles Howard Candler, former president of the Coca-Cola Company, and now the Callanwolde Fine Arts Center.

40 Lake Lanier Islands, a paradise for water-sports, are four state-administered islands, 1,200 recreational acres with camping, swimming, tennis, picknicking, sailing, horseback riding and fishing and a range of accommodation from cottage and houseboat to hotel.

41 *(right)* Dillard, near Ski Valley; Georgia's mountains offer panoramic trail-hiking in summer and excellent skiing in winter.

42 Westin Peachtree Plaza, the world's tallest hotel (73 stories), a circular tower that dominates the skyline; the multi-storey atrium lobby contains a half-acre lake with 'cocktail islands' and one of the hotel's restaurants has a waterfall 100 feet deep.

43 *(right)* University of Georgia Stadium, Athens campus.

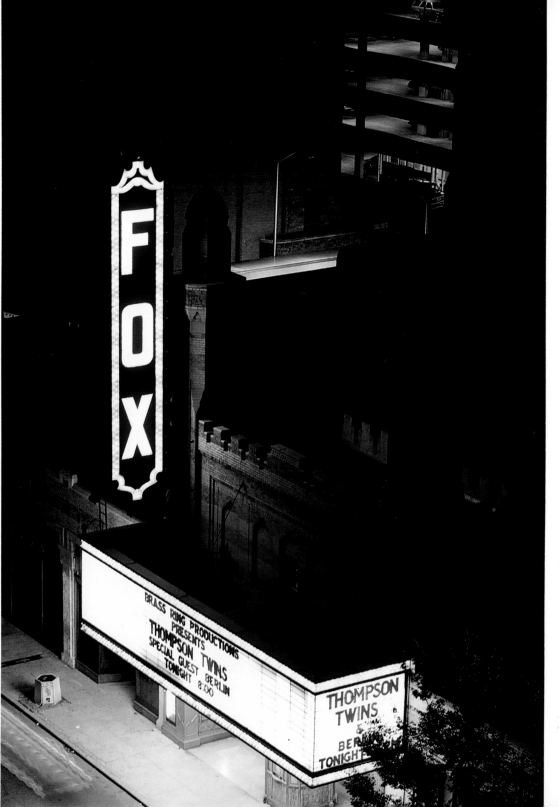

44 The Fox Theatre has a 4,000-seat auditorium modelled on a Moorish courtyard, its stage complete with twinkling stars, sunrise, sunset and moving clouds. Built in 1929 for a Shrine temple, it has functioned mostly as a movie-palace, second in size only to Radio City Music Hall, New York. Today the Fox offers a wide range, including concerts, ballet and theatre as well as movies, and is one of the few theatres recognized as a National Landmark.

45 *(right)* 'Limelight' is a multi-faceted complex of disco, dining, night-club and movie entertainment.

46 *(left)* Excelsior Mill, a reminder of the industrial past.

47 Hartsfield Atlanta International Airport has the largest passenger terminal in the world, employs 30,000 people, making it the largest private employer in Georgia, and has plans to expand the present handling facilities to 75 million passengers a year.

48 Rubber-rafting on the Chattahoochee River, through the Chattahoochee National Recreation Area.

49 *(right)* Balloon race in Piedmont Park.

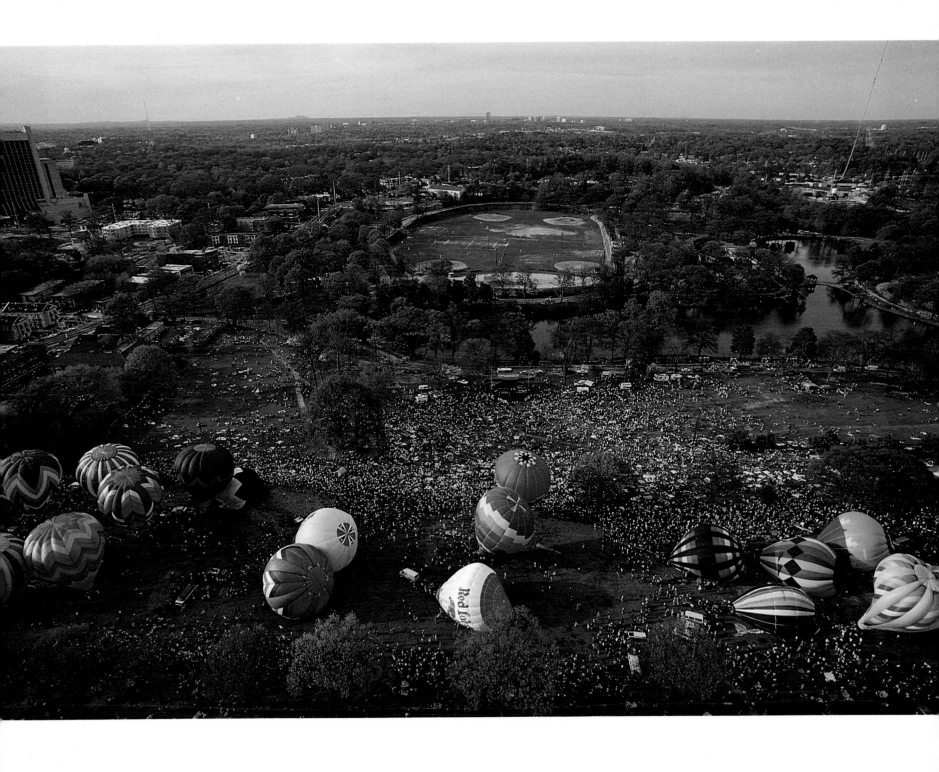

50 Antique water-wheel, Berry College.

51 Etowah Indian Mounds, near Cartersville; with the huge burial mounds at Ocmulgee near Macon and the Kolomoki Mounds near Blakely, these are among the archaeological keys to knowledge of inhabitants of the region over 5,000 years ago.

52 *(left)* Downtown, with the tower of the Westin Peachtree Plaza.

53 The Atlanta Botanical Garden, Piedmont Park, includes a conservatory, a Japanese garden, a formal herb garden and a rose garden; shown here (clockwise from top-left), magnolia, rose, dogwood and hibiscus.

54 The Tullie Smith House is an authentic Georgia farmhouse and out-
buildings, restored to the 1840s and now maintained by the Atlanta
Historical Society.

UNLAWFUL TO PARK WAGON OR BUGGIES AROUND THIS SQUARE

THIS MARKER WAS PLACED ON THIS CORNER IN 1900, AND WAS RECONDITIONED IN 1944 BY DECATUR LIONS CLUB

55 Warning sign beside the Decatur Town Square Station of the ultra-modern MARTA (Metropolitan Atlanta Rapid Transit Authority—see plate 73).

56 CNN Cable Television News, Turner Communications.

57 *(right)* The Omni Coliseum, a 16,000-seat indoor sports-palace, home
of the NBA Hawks basketball team and also the setting for ice shows,
circuses, concerts and many other events.

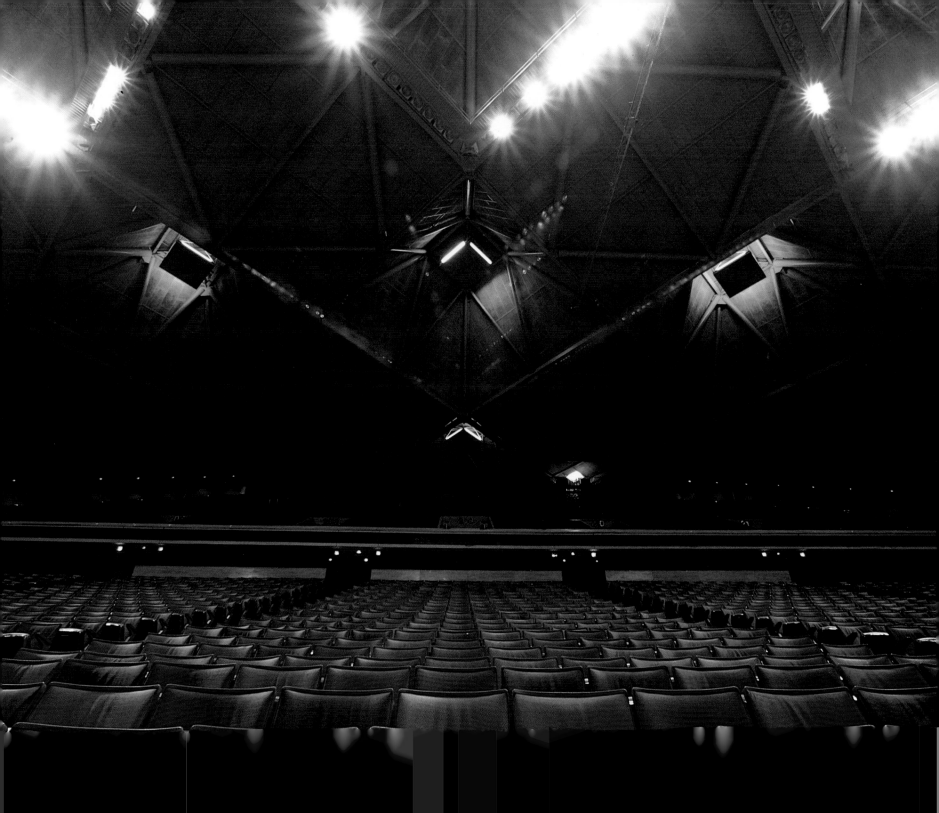

58 Altar, Church of the Sacred Heart.

59 *(right)* Shrine of the Immaculate Conception.

60 & 61 Atlanta has three excellent public golf-courses and the largest lawn-tennis association in America.

62 & 63 4th July Parade.

64 *(left)* Sunset from the rooftop of the Ramada Hotel.

65 Atlanta seen from the rooftop of the Coca-Cola Building.

66 *(left)* Dogwood in blossom; the annual Atlanta Dogwood Festival is one of Georgia's most attractive spring events.

67 Springtime along Habersham Drive, in a beautiful residential area of Atlanta with some of Georgia's most elegant homes and gardens.

68 The Peachtree Plaza tower with the
Coastal States Building in the background.

69 *(right)* Oakland Cemetery; one of the out-
s nding arrays of Victorian monuments (see
plate 12). Oakland is the last resting-place of
many Confederates and Unionists alike, as
well as six Governors of Georgia, twenty-
three Mayors of Atlanta, the golfer Bobby
Jones and Margaret Mitchell Marsh, author
of *Gone with the Wind*.

70 Lenox Square Mall.

71 'The Varsity' Drive-In, opened in 1928, has become an institution in
itself; this enormous fast-food outlet, famous for its chili-dogs, is reputed
to serve as many as 10,000 hamburgers and 15,000 hot-dogs in one day.

72 Plaza Drugs, a well-known 24-hour pharmacy.

73 (right) MARTA North Station; the Metropolitan Atlanta Rapid Transit Authority is an integrated bus and rail network, the buses covering nearly 2,000 miles of streets and the rapid-rail services extending beyond the city on an east-west monorail line. The stations are outstanding examples of urban-transit design and are decorated with brilliant murals.

74 Dahlonega; here in 1828 occurred America's first gold-rush and from Dahlonega comes the old saying 'Thar's gold in them thar hills!' Dahlonega provided the gold to cover the dome of the State Capitol (see plate 76).

75 *(right)* Stone Mountain, the world's largest single exposed mass of granite (see also plates 17, 20, 28, 29) is 825 feet high and some 290 million years old.

76 *(left)* The State Capitol of Georgia (1889) houses the Georgia State Museum of Science and Industry, a Hall of Fame and a Hall of Flags, as well as the offices and chambers of government. In 1958 the dome was covered with gold-leaf from Dahlonega (see plate 74).

77 Fourth of July Parade; those who still come to Atlanta looking for Scarlett O'Hara might just be lucky on this occasion.

REV. MARTIN LUTHER KING, JR.

1929 — 1968

"Free at last, Free at last,
Thank God Almighty
I'm Free at last."

78 Martin Luther King Jr Historic District; the Nobel Prize winner and leader of the civil rights movement is entombed here beside the Ebenezer Baptist Church where he used to preach, close to his birthplace and surrounded by the Freedom Hall Complex, home of the Martin Luther King Jr Center for Nonviolent Social Change.

79 *(right)* The Swan House, built in 1928 as a private mansion for Mr and Mrs Edward H. Inman of the Inman railroad family, in the Palladian style, with beautiful boxwood gardens; now a museum furnished with precious antiques and maintained by the Atlanta Historical Society. Swan motifs decorate the building throughout.

80 Dillard, N. Georgia (see plates 14 and 41).

81 *(right)* Knickerbocker's Restaurant and Bar, another good example of the recycling and restoration of an old building.

a

b

82 (left) a) Hank Aaron, of the Atlanta Braves, and b) a fan of the Braves.

83 NL Baseball Atlanta Braves in action.

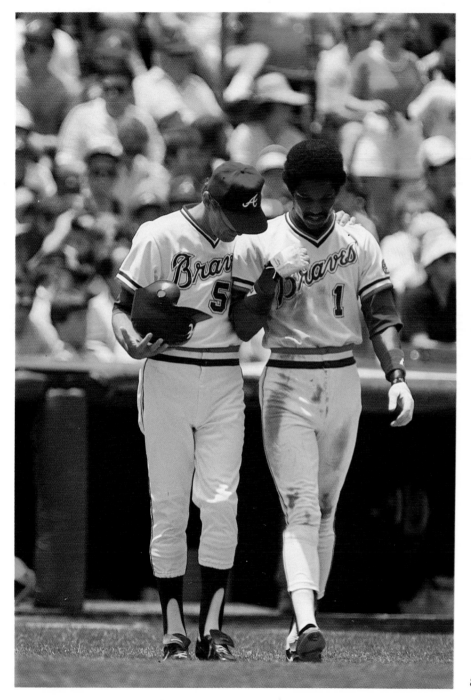

84 & 85 More scenes from NL Baseball Atlanta Braves' game.

86 *(left)* Atlanta/Fulton County Stadium (with up to 60,000 seats), home of the NL baseball's Braves and the NFL football's Atlanta Falcons.

87 Balloon race over Atlanta.

88 Atlanta, 'Gate City of the South', and 'Next International City of the World'.